# KEW AS IT WAS

by

## G. E. Cassidy

Chairman
The Richmond Society History Section

"A village set around its modest Chapel,
Fronting the velvet pasture of the Green;
Here in the halcyon days of England's summer
Noble and commoner alike are seen
In manly sport and emulation keen."

*Anon.*

**1.** *Front Cover:* The north side of Kew Green in 1910 showing the old Rose and Crown and the tea houses which were then a feature of the village. The Ivy Hotel, Burton's Restaurant which was later Pitt's, the Dieudonne and the Imperial are seen with awnings covering their front gardens.

*First edition, October 1982*
*Second Impression, May 1985*

*Published by Hendon Publishing Company Limited, Hendon Mill, Nelson, Lancashire*
*Text © G. E. Cassidy, 1982*
*Printed by Fretwell & Brian Ltd., Goulbourne Street, Keighley, West Yorkshire*

# THE VILLAGE OF KEW

Kew is famous the world over because of the Royal Botanic Gardens but it is also a village of great charm with a fascinating history and is distinguished for its royal connections. It was first mentioned during the reign of King Henry VII, in the Court Rolls of the Manor of Richmond, by the name 'Kai-Hoo' (a landing place by the waterside).

The village grew up around several large houses occupied by members of the Court, the place being convenient to the royal palaces at Richmond and Hampton Court and easily accessible from London by way of the River Thames. One of these houses, Kew House or the White House, which stood opposite the present Kew Palace, was leased in 1728 from the Capel family by Frederick, Prince of Wales, as his country residence. He and his wife, Princess Augusta, encouraged by their friend, the Earl of Bute, transformed the house and established the garden which eventually became the Royal Botanic Gardens. It was in the White House, known then as Kew Palace, that their son King George III spent much of his long reign and during this period many houses were built around the Green for members of the royal household.

The church was built in 1714, the first Kew Bridge in 1758 and it was then that the village assumed the form which it retained for more than a century. This was changed dramatically by the coming of the railway in about 1860. Thereafter the land to the east of the Green, the Priory Estate, was laid out with new roads and lines of terrace houses. The area between the railway and the road to Richmond was developed with many new roads and large houses for the carriage folk, business men from Richmond and London. In a few years the village had more than doubled in size.

Between the two world wars, Kew itself changed little, but beyond the railway, to the east, a vast new area of housing came into being, covering all the original market garden lands.

After the Second World War Kew, like so many other places, went through a period of social change, reflected in the replacement of many of the large Victorian houses by blocks of flats or town houses and by infilling with small dwellings. The appearance of the heart of the village, around the Green has, however, changed little and happily retains its eighteenth century character.

**2.** *A VIEW OF KEW,* from a well known print of about 1765, shows, with much artist's licence, St Anne's Church as originally constructed, the first Kew Bridge and the Pagoda. It shows also the road which ran across the middle of the Green, between the White House and the Dutch House and on to Brentford Ferry. Driving along it is the King's coach with an escort of Life Guards on its way to cross Kew Bridge.

**3. THE WHITE HOUSE,** formerly known as Kew House and later Kew Palace was owned in the middle of the seventeenth century by Richard Bennet, a London merchant whose father was Lord Mayor. On his death it passed to his daughter, the wife of Sir Henry Capel who was later raised to the peerage and became Lord Deputy of Ireland. After his death in 1696, the house passed to Samuel Molyneux, who had married his grand-niece and was an intimate of the royal family, having been secretary to George II when he was Prince of Wales. He was a talented astronomer and at Kew he set up a telescope by means of which the famous Dr Bradley made the observations which led to the discovery of the 'aberration of light'. In 1728 he leased the house to Frederick, Prince of Wales, who had it remodelled by William Kent in the severe classical style shown in this print. It became the country residence of George III who spent much time at Kew, living in the style of a country gentleman. It was, however, too small for the very large royal family and it became dilapidated and was demolished in 1802.

**4. KEW PALACE** c. 1878. The sixteenth century building on the site of the present Kew Palace was known as the Dairie House and was leased to the Earl of Leicester, favourite of Queen Elizabeth I. It was later occupied by the Portman family and in 1630 was purchased by Samuel Fortrey, a London merchant of Flemish descent. He rebuilt the house completely in Dutch style and it is a fine example of ornamental brickwork. Early in the eighteenth century it was leased to the Crown and used to house visitors to the Palace and the many children of George III. After the King's death, his Queen, Charlotte, lived there until her own death in 1818. It was later incorporated into the Gardens and was opened to the public in 1899.

**5. KEW PALACE** — the rear view before the colonnade and balcony were restored and the Queen's Garden created in 1969.

**6. THE CASTLELLATED PALACE.** King George III long cherished the ambition to build a fine castle at Kew to replace the dilapidated and inconvenient White House. In 1800, James Wyatt, the distinguished architect, was commissioned to design this building and work began in 1801. The stone castle was in a romantic, gothic style and was built in two stages. First the main body of the house, 100 feet square and with battlemented turrets, and then a huge forecourt with symmetrical flanking offices, fully furnished also with an array of battlements. The work, which cost more than half a million pounds, all taken from the Privy Purse, was never completed and the King's final madness in 1811 brought the building programme to a halt. The half-finished shell was an object of public scorn for years until it was blown up in 1827–8.

Described as a 'singular monument of eccentricity and expense' the castle was remarkable for its form of construction, being one of the first buildings ever to be supported on cast iron columns.

# THE ROYAL BOTANIC GARDENS

The famous gardens at Kew as we now know them were formed by the joining together, in the mid eighteenth century, of two considerable royal properties. The western or riverside half was part of the grounds of Ormonde Lodge, residence of King George II, which stood in the Old Deer Park and was demolished in 1772. The garden had been laid out in the style fashionable at the time by Queen Caroline and embellished with exotic follies such as Merlin's Cave and The Hermitage, which have not survived.

The eastern half was the estate attached to the White House, which stood opposite to the present Kew Palace. When this was leased in 1728 by Frederick, Prince of Wales, it already had a notable garden, established by Lord Capel and praised by the diarist, Evelyn. Encouraged by their friend the Earl of Bute, a passionate gardener and student of botany, the Prince and his wife, Augusta, developed this garden which was extended from 7 acres to double that size.

It was converted into a truly 'botanic' garden with a fine collection of unusual and exotic plants. William Kent was appointed to design the layout and improve the house, William Chambers to act as architect and William Aiton to deal with the practical work in the gardens. To Chambers we owe the classical Orangery and the various temples and the famous Pagoda which expressed the great interest of the age in things exotic and oriental.

It was King George III who linked these two gardens together by closing the road which ran between them. To the charge of the great new garden he appointed the young Joseph Banks and he began the practice of sending collectors to all parts of the world to obtain plants for Kew. Thus was laid the foundation of the collection of plants and herbarium material for which Kew is so well known. After the death in 1820 of both George III and Joseph Banks, Kew was neglected for many years and there was danger that, with diminishing royal interest, the unique collection might well be lost. However, in 1841, the gardens came under public control with Sir William Hooker as the first official Director. He was succeeded in 1865 by his son, Joseph, and in half a century these two remarkable and devoted men created the world famous horticultural and scientific institution which the Royal Botanic Gardens has since remained.

**7 and 8.**   ENTRANCE GATES.   In about 1825 the road across Kew Green which led down between the White House and the Dutch House (the two Kew Palaces) to Brentford Ferry, was closed and the Gardens were extended northwards to the river. The new boundary ran across the Green on the line of the avenue known as 'Birdcage Walk' and in the centre were erected the entrance gates flanked by stone lodges. By order of King William IV the boundary was moved further west to restore to the people of Kew the use of the western end of the Green. In 1845 the splendid semi-circular entrance screen and gates were erected on the new boundary line to the design of Decimus Burton, architect of the Temperate House and the Palm House. The Lion and Unicorn, originally on the lodges, can still be seen over the Lion and Unicorn Gates in Kew Road.

**9.  PAGODA VISTA.**   A view from the top of the Pagoda, looking north along Pagoda Vista, at the turn of the century and showing, much less veiled in trees than now, the Temperate House, Palm House, Marianne North Gallery and the refreshment pavilion. Not only the lengthening shadows of the trees suggest that it is tea time.

**10.  THE OUTING.**  A visit to Kew has long been a traditional feature of English life. Here is an early Edwardian family enjoying the scent of a great bed of roses in the Gardens.

**11.  THE TEMPLE OF THE SUN.**  One of the most delightful of the buildings designed by Sir William Chambers to adorn the 'botanic' garden of Princess Augusta was the Temple of the Sun. This was built in 1761 and was more richly decorated than the other buildings. In full Corinthian style it was enriched on the outside with a finely moulded frieze and had an internal frieze with a sunburst and the signs of the zodiac. Alongside it and, as it happened, too close, was planted a cedar of Lebanon and in a great storm in March 1916 this tree was blown over onto the temple which was completely destroyed.

**12. THE PALM HOUSE.** For much more than a century the Palm House has been one of the outstanding features of the Gardens. This magnificent glasshouse (or Great Stove) was built at the instigation of Sir William Hooker and was completed in 1848. It was designed by the architect Decimus Burton, in an uneasy collaboration with Richard Turner, an iron founder from Dublin, and was for a long time the largest and most spectacular palm house in the world.

**13. THE REFRESHMENT PAVILION** in about 1910. The original refreshment pavilion, built in the 'Swiss Chalet' style, was notable for having been burnt down, in February 1913, by two suffragettes. They had previously damaged the Orchid House to draw attention to their campaign for 'votes for women'. A new pavilion was erected in 1915.

FIRE BRIGADES. For many years Kew Palace boasted its own fire brigade.

**14.** Here is the splendid engine of 1885.

**15.** Here is the brigade of 1923, posing with the Director, Sir Arthur Hill.

**16. THE CONSTABLES OF KEW.** Sir William Thistleton-Dyer, son-in-law of Joseph Hooker, was Director of the Gardens from 1885 to 1905. A brilliant and energetic botanist and scientist, he did as much as anyone in the development of the Gardens, but he was something of an eccentric. He had a passion for uniforms and ordered that the staff should wear at all times the uniforms which he himself designed. He had himself appointed Inspector of Constables so that he could strut about the gardens in splendour. Here he is seen with the constables in 1905, posing before King William's Temple.

**17. QUEEN MARY AT KEW.** Queen Mary, whose parents the Duke and Duchess of Teck, were married in St. Anne's Church, was always fond of Kew. Here she is seen at the Entrance Gates on one of her many visits to the Gardens.

**18, 19, 20 and 21.** KEW CHURCH. The parish church of St. Anne was built in 1714 on land on Kew Green presented by Queen Anne, who also gave £100 towards the cost. It was originally a very small building comprising only a nave, 64 ft. by 27 ft., with 24 pews and a gallery. It was enlarged in 1770 at the expense of King George III to the design of Joshua Kirby, Teacher in Perspective and Clerk of Works to the royal household, the nave being lengthened and the north and south aisles added. The latter was separated from the nave and used as a charity school house and lodging for the Beadle. In 1810 the south aisle was embodied in the church. In 1836 the west end was remodelled at the expense of King William IV to the designs of Sir William Wyatville and in 1884 the south porch and the fine domed chancel were added.

# THE THREE KEW BRIDGES

For many generations there were two ferries across the River Thames at Kew. The horse ferry was continuous with the line of Smith's Hill, Brentford and Ealing Lane and the foot ferry followed roughly the line of the present bridge. In the reign of Charles I the right of the horse ferry was made by royal grant to a royalist, Mr Thornton. After the King's execution, an opposition ferry was established by a Commonwealth supporter, Mr Tunstall, but on the restoration he was forced to give this up. A little later, however, he purchased the right from Mr Thornton and the ferry continued in his family for another hundred years.

**22.** THE FIRST KEW BRIDGE.   The Tunstalls were prosperous businessmen from Brentford and in 1757, Robert, the then owner of the ferry, obtained by Act of Parliament consent for the building of a bridge at or near the ferry site. Objections from bargemasters that this would interfere with the navigation of the river resulted in a new site being chosen, on the line of the foot ferry, known as Powel's. The bridge was begun on 29th April 1758 and completed by the end of May 1759. It consisted of eleven arches, the two at each end being of brick and stone and the seven in the centre of timber. The centre arch had a span of 50 ft. and the roadway was 30 ft. wide. On the 1st June 1759 the Prince of Wales (later George III), the Princess Dowager and the royal family passed over the new bridge and it was opened for traffic on the 4th June, the Prince's birthday. During the day 3000 people went across the bridge. To mark the occasion there was a large meeting of gentlemen of the neighbourhood, who dined together at the Rose and Crown. In the evening there was a bonfire and illuminations on Kew Green.

**23, 24 and 25.   THE SECOND KEW BRIDGE.** The first bridge, being made mostly of timber, did not last long, only just outliving its founder. His son, another Robert Tunstall, found that the costs of the repairs required to the rickety structure were greater than the tolls would cover. In 1782, therefore, he obtained consent by Act of Parliament for a new stone bridge, to be built a hundred feet or so east of the old one. This was a handsome bridge of seven arches designed by James Paine, who also designed Richmond Bridge. Robert Tunstall was joined in the enterprise by John Haverfield II and by Charles Brown, a carpenter. Work was commenced on 4th June 1783, the King's birthday, and completed on 22nd September 1789, when the bridge was opened for traffic. Tolls were charged, ½d for each foot passenger and 6d for each horse. The bridge was purchased in 1819 by a Mr Robinson for £22,000. In 1873 the tolls were extinguished when the bridge was purchased for £57,300 by a joint committee of the Corporation of London and the Metropolitan Board of Works.

**26.   THE THIRD KEW BRIDGE.**   The second Kew Bridge lasted for 110 years but by 1899 it had become 'absurdly inadequate for modern requirements' by reason of the narrowness of the carriageway and its steepness at the centre. It was, therefore, closed and a temporary bridge of timber built on the west side for use while the old bridge was demolished and the new one erected. This was undertaken by the County Councils of Surrey and Middlesex at a cost of £250,000. This most handsome bridge, with its three great elliptical arches, each spanning over 100 ft., was designed by Sir John Wolfe Barry and Cuthbert Brereton and built by Messrs Easton Gibb & Son. It was opened by King Edward VII in the afternoon of the 20th May 1903 with the most elaborate ceremonial. In a pavilion erected at the centre of the bridge the King laid the last coping stone using a silver trowel, the handle being made of wood from a pile from the old bridge. Among many gifts presented to the King was an axe-head, mounted in gold, which had been found in the river bed during the excavations. After the royal party had returned to London by way of Barnes village and Putney Bridge, there was a reception in the grounds of Kew Palace, 1000 children were given tea in a marquee on Kew Green and a civic banquet was held at the Star and Garter Hotel, Richmond.

**27.   THE OPENING OF THE THIRD KEW BRIDGE.   When King Edward VII came to Kew in 1903 to open the new bridge he was warmly received by the people of Brentford and welcomed at the north end of the bridge by a splendid guard of honour mounted by the Middlesex Imperial Yeomanry, the 2nd Battalion of the Duke of Cambridge's Own Middlesex Regiment with band and the 2nd Volunteer Battalion of the same regiment.**

**28.** THE TOLL HOUSES OF THE SECOND KEW BRIDGE.   As originally designed by James Paine the second Kew Bridge was to have been a most ornate structure, meant to be the finest in the land. The Toll Houses would have been richly embellished with pedimented doric style porticoes and sculptured groups. For reasons of economy the scheme had to be drastically modified and it was these modest buildings which served until the tolls were extinguished in 1873.

**29.** 57–61 KEW GREEN IN 1903.   No. 57, Hanover House, at the left, was the home of
Jeremiah Meyer, miniaturist and medallist, one of the founders of the Royal Academy, who
designed the new coinage for George III in 1761. The little road alongside, originally called Water
Lane, became known as Meyer's Lane and after 1823 became Ferry Lane. The house was
subsequently occupied by senior members of the Kew Gardens staff. No. 61, Abingdon Lodge (later
Abingdon House), was occupied by Joshua and Sarah Kirby. Kirby came to Kew in 1759 as Teacher
in Perspective to the Prince of Wales and his family. He was appointed Clerk of Works to the royal
household and was architect for the enlargement of St. Anne's Church in 1770. He was a great
friend of Meyer and Gainsborough and father of Mrs Trimmer, the celebrated writer of children's
books and founder of the Sunday School movement.

**30.** 61 and 63 KEW GREEN IN THE TWENTIES. From the late nineteenth century these houses were in use as tea houses serving the many visitors to Kew Gardens. In 1913, Will Evans came to Kew and among other houses took over No. 61 as the Imperial Restaurant. No. 63, then known as Snailwell House, was badly damaged by fire in 1919 and was restored and reopened by Will Evans as the Dieudonne Restaurant.

**31.** THE TEA GARDENS. The spacious tea gardens at the rear of the Imperial and the Dieudonne restaurants are here seen in their heyday in the 1930s with the proud proprietor, Will Evans, in the foreground.

**32. 77 KEW GREEN.** Beaconsfield, which was always known as The Little Red House, is one of the oldest houses in Kew and was built in 1668. It was for a time the home of Mr Albert, who came to England with Queen Charlotte as a royal page. He was the father of the celebrated Mrs Papendiek, whose journals tell us so much about life in the household of George III. The house was owned by Francis Engleheart, the modeller of plaster ceilings and first of the family of artists so closely connected with Kew. It was later occupied by Mrs Clementina Schnell, daughter of Colonel Macdonald, a friend of Bonny Prince Charlie. She claimed to be the goddaughter of the Old Pretender and was said to be something of a bore. She lived in The Little Red House for fifty years and met her death in an accident when she set fire to her crinoline and ornate headdress.

**33. THE ROSE AND CROWN.** Always one of the principal inns of the village, the old Rose and Crown was well known in the Georgian period for its spacious banqueting rooms. These were the scene of some notable celebrations. Among these were the banquet held on the 4th June 1759 to mark the opening of the first Kew Bridge and the great Ball and Supper on the 25th October 1809 to commemorate the fiftieth anniversary of the accession of King George III.

**34.** **84 KEW GREEN.** Flora House was built in 1880 as a private residence until, like almost all the houses on the north side of the Green, it became a tea house. It was one of the properties purchased by Will Evans in 1913 and it was here he lived for the rest of his life. Here we see some of the staff posing in the trellised entrance to Flora Restaurant.

**35.** Nos. 87 and 89 KEW GREEN, 1899. These two houses stood at the foot of Kew Bridge on the west side of the approach and were for many years occupied by members of the Pring family—William Pring, senior, having been landlord of the adjoining King's Arms from as far back as 1850. No. 87, Thames House was used as builders' offices and No. 89 was a sweetshop. They were demolished in 1900 when the third Kew Bridge was being erected. They are seen here awaiting demolition, No. 87 being the office of the Resident Engineer for the bridge works while No. 89 stands empty.

**36. KEW GREEN ABOUT 1898.** This view, looking north along Kew Road just before the second Kew Bridge was closed, shows the narrowness and steepness of the bridge which made it unsuitable for the heavy traffic of the time. On the right hand side is the old forge and a horse tram standing at the terminus. On the left hand side is the old King's Arms, of which Mr Sadler was then the landlord and alongside it No. 87, Kew Green, Thames House, offices of Warden and Pring, builders and No. 89, Miss Pring's tea house and sweet shop.

**37. THE OLD FORGE.** The original Rose and Crown Inn stood at the foot of Kew Bridge on the east side and it was moved to its present site in the eighteenth century. From then on the old building was used as a blacksmith's shop as shown in this photograph taken in September 1899. It was demolished soon afterwards when the present bridge was built. The cottage next door still remains as part of commercial premises.

**38. KEW GREEN IN 1903.**
A view from the foot of Kew Bridge, looking southward along Kew Road towards the church.

**39. and 40.** CHURCH COTTAGES, 1928. Nos. 1–7 Kew Green, Church Cottages, were built in 1710 and for many years formed a sort of shopping centre for the village. They were purchased by the Council in 1929 together with part of the garden of Descanso House, and demolished for the widening of Kew Road and the Mortlake Road junction. They were specially notable for their connection with the Taylor family. The Taylors were originally prosperous Surrey landowners with business connections with the City. In the late eighteenth century their fortunes declined and they turned to trade. They came to Kew where they lived in Nos. 1 and 3 Church Cottages and also what is now 21 Kew Green. They set up a bakery and post office, Henry Taylor being the first postmaster in Kew some fifty years before postage stamps were invented. Six generations of Taylors lived in Kew and served the village for nearly two centuries.

**41.   KING'S COTTAGE, 1903.**   No. 33 Kew Green was built in the early eighteenth century and was used by the Earl of Bute, who lived next door at Cambridge Cottage, as a study and to house his herbarium and magnificent horticultural library. It was the home of Princess Elizabeth, one of the daughters of George III, and was long known as Princess Elizabeth's House. When she left, the Colonel commanding the household troops had lodgings there, convenient to the barracks just along the Green. It was for a time the residence of the Vicar of Kew when it was called Church House. Subsequently it became a Grace and Favour house and was occupied in turn by the Infanta Beatrice of Spain, Archbishop Lord Lang and the Marquess of Carisbrooke.

# NOTABLE EVENTS ON KEW GREEN

**42.  FUNERAL OF THE DUKE OF CAMBRIDGE.**
Adolphus Frederick, Duke of Cambridge, youngest son of George III, was brought up in Kew and after a period of service as Viceroy of Hanover returned to live in his cottage on Kew Green. When he died in London in July 1850 at the age of 76 his body was taken first to Hanover House and thence to Cambridge Cottage. In the funeral procession to the church the coffin was carried by twelve colour sergeants of the Coldstream Guards and the service was attended by the Prince Consort, the Duke of Wellington, Lord Palmerston and many other gentlemen. The body was laid in the church and later interred in the mausoleum built at the east end. From there it was removed to Windsor in 1930.

**43.  TRIUMPHAL ARCH.**  William IV was a great benefactor of Kew. Not only did he extend the Green and improve the church by the rebuilding of the west front but, in 1836, he graciously made 200 seats in the church free for the use of the people. On 19th September 1836 he visited Kew for the fourth time that summer and the people of the village showed their gratitude and loyalty by holding a splendid fete. A triumphal arch, tastefully decorated with evergreens, dahlias, asters and other autumnal flowers was erected across the main road. In a tent 100 ft long the schoolchildren were regaled with roast beef and plum pudding; the usual cricket match between married and single took place and in the evening there were illuminations and a firework display. The arch was designed by|the |Revd. T. Tunstall Haverfield, son of John Haverfield II and curate of St. Anne's. Prominent in the design were the initials of the King and his Queen Adelaide while the several white ensigns must have been specially pleasing to the 'sailor king'.

**44.  THE WEDDING OF THE DUKE OF TECK.**   A joyous occasion for the people of Kew was the wedding, on the 12th June 1866, of Princess Mary Adelaide, daughter of the Duke of Cambridge and cousin of Queen Victoria, to H.S.H. the Duke of Teck. The popular Princess Mary was married from her home, Cambridge Cottage, and for the procession to the church the path was strewn with flowers by the children of the local parish schools. The ceremony was conducted by the Archbishop of Canterbury and the vicar, the Revd. R. B. Byam. It was attended by Queen Victoria, in heavy mourning for her late Consort. A great floral arch was erected across the road at the foot of Kew Bridge through which the newly married couple drove on their way to London.

**45. THE EASTER FAIR.** For many years a great fair was held along the north side of Kew Green on Easter Monday, with stalls selling all sorts of wares to tempt the visitors to the Gardens. In addition to the purveyors of whelks and teas and patent medicines there were sideshows, Punch and Judy shows and a variety of kerbside entertainment. Because of the local by-laws of the time the stallholders were not allowed to cross Kew Bridge before a certain time in the early morning. So they lined up on the Middlesex side of the centre of the bridge, marshalled by the police, and at a given signal raced with their carts and barrows down the slope of the bridge to secure the best pitches on the greenside. This provided great entertainment for the local children. This view is of one of the last of the fairs to be held, just before the Second World War.

**46. THE MORNING AFTER.** The scale of the Easter Fairs can be judged by the amount of litter left behind. These lovely eighteenth century houses, formerly the homes of Georgian courtiers, seem to be trying to ignore the indignity of the scene before them and to resent being used as tea houses.

**47.   THE OLDE ENGLISHE FAYRE.**   A spectacular event on Kew Green was the Olde Englishe Fayre held on the 22nd July 1914. For this occasion the Green was filled with tents and stalls and the events included Old English dancing, boxing, band concerts and first and foremost a fabulous fancy dress parade. For this no less than 300 local children appeared in a wide range of costumes which were judged by the well known actress Miss Ethel Irving. A feature of the event was the use of Mr Pitt's restaurant which formed Ye Olde English Garden where teas were served in vast quantity. In the evening a gala concert was given in a pavilion specially erected in the garden. At this concert a child pupil of Mr Warner, the organist, gave a superb piano recital and Miss Margaret Cooper entertained with her 'dainty chansons'. The evening closed with a torchlight tattoo by the London Irish Rifles.

**48.**   Lord Lonsdale had been invited to open the Fayre but was unable to be present. Mr George Cave, the Member of Parliament, was detained at the House of Commons so the opening ceremony was performed, as it was reported, 'with his usual dignified eloquence' by the well loved vicar of Kew, the Revd. W. H. Bliss. He is seen wearing his Victoria Jubilee medal and the coronation medals of King Edward and King George.

"Olde Englishe Fayre" Kew Green, 22nd July 1914.

J.B. Milnes
Series 3694.

# SPORT ON KEW GREEN

**49.  FOOTBALL.**   This is the St. Anne's Church football club in 1910 – part of the Church Boy's Club founded in 1906 by a great man of the village, Kenneth Leatherdale, second from the left in the back row. He also founded the successful Kew Association Football Club which is still flourishing. In the early years they played on the field alongside the river close to the railway bridge, owned by Mr A. Ladbrook and now the Priory Park Sports Club.

**50. CRICKET.** Cricket on the Green seems always to have been an important feature of the life of Kew. The first match recorded was played in 1737 between the Prince of Wales' team and a team of Gentlemen from London, for a purse of 100 guineas. Needless to say the Prince's team won. Organised cricket has been played from at least 1824 and a banquet to celebrate the centenary of the first Kew Cricket Club was held in the Dieudonne in 1924. The club in its present form dates from 1882. In this scene of about 1910 the wicket is seen pitched east and west instead of north and south as at present.

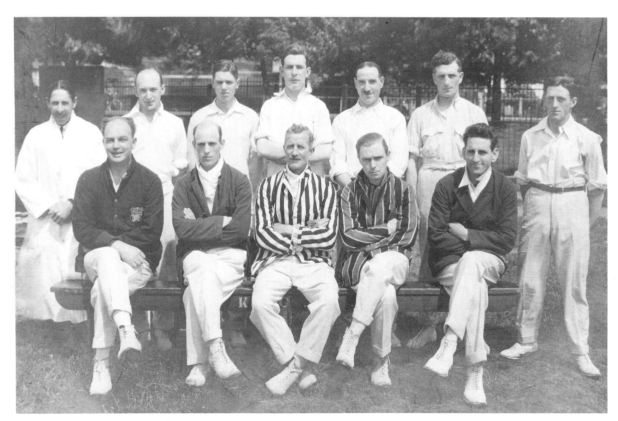

**51.** This group of players in 1924 includes some well known Kew cricketing characters—Alf Pring, the umpire, Jim Finch, a superb slow bowler, Oxford Keene, one of the big hitters of the day and Sandy Mulford, a fine all rounder.

**52.   KEW BOYS ANNUAL CRICKET MATCH.**   A regular cricketing event on Kew Green was for many years the Kew Boys Annual Cricket Match. This was founded in 1881 by William Pring, senior, landlord of the King's Arms and continued for something like 90 years. The boys of the village were divided into two teams, not necessarily with the usual eleven players, and the teams were traditionally known as Oxford and Cambridge. They wore dark and light blue ribbons and were provided with the clothes and equipment suitable to the occasion. Prizes were presented for the best performances in batting, bowling and fielding and a splendid tea was provided. The cost of the event was met by public subscription and everyone taking part was given a group photograph as a memento of the occasion. This is the photograph of 1903 showing the beribboned players, officials and committee.

**53.   KEW GREEN.**
A view of the Green in about 1905 looking northward from the Mortlake Road junction.

**54. KEW ROAD IN 1895.** This view of Kew Road, looking north towards the Mortlake Road junction, shows the narrowness of the road at this point, with its single tramway line. In 1917 the cottages on the right were acquired by the Council for £1000 and demolished for the widening of the road. Twinn's, the greengrocer's shop, later became the office and yard of Mr Horwill, the builder.

**55. GLOUCESTER COTTAGES IN 1899.** Built in the late eighteenth century to house workers in Kew Gardens, Nos. 320–332 Kew Road later housed a number of small businesses. H. Hiscock has a sign offering his services as a private gardener while Mr James' refreshment rooms offer a wide range of soft and alcoholic drinks, confectionary, teas at 6d and 'Good lock-ups for bicycles'.

**56. GLOUCESTER HOUSE IN 1909.** No. 334 Kew Road, known as Gloucester House, was built in 1750 and was used as an occasional country residence by the Duke of Gloucester, brother of George III. The cottage alongside was occupied by his equerry, Colonel Speed. When the Duke died in 1805 the house was taken over by the younger Mr Aiton, head gardener at Kew, and he lived there until moving to Windsor. After a short occupancy by a clergyman named Vine the house was purchased, in 1840, by an aristocratic Portugese Jew, Mr Neumegen. Mr and Mrs Neumegen established a very high class boarding school for Jewish boys and girls. Mr Neumegen died long before his wife who continued to run the school well into the present century. Their daughter continued with the school until the end of the First World War. From 1921 to 1934 the house, which had by then been much altered, was used as a Labour Party College. It was finally demolished to make way for one of the first developments of flats in Kew, Gloucester Court.

**57.  NEWENS.**   Newens Bakery has been famous for many years and known the world over for 'Maids of Honour', those delicious tarts with an almond flavoured filling, the recipe for which is a closely guarded secret. The founder, Alfred Nachbar Newens, opened his first shop in George Street, Richmond but very soon moved to the present shop in Kew Road in 1880. Since then the business has been continued by four generations of the Newens family. Here, Alfred Newens and his family and staff are posed in front of the original Kew shop, which was largely rebuilt after the Second World War in which it was badly damaged by bombing. Mrs Newens stands to the left of Alfred; on his right is his son Frank, who distinguished himself as a photographer, and his daughter Kathleen who, with John, who is holding the pony, continued in the business all her life.

**58.   DELIVERING THE BREAD**

**59.   KEW SCOUTS.**   The Kew Scout Troop was founded in 1909 as the 2nd Richmond. They are seen here manning a Merryweather manual Fire Engine. This appliance had been donated by J. Compton Merryweather 'so that fire drill may become a recognised and active part of the training of Boy Scouts'. Holding the hose is Patrol Leader Reg Bowden, who was a founder member of the troop.

# FLOODS

The village of Kew has been flooded many times. It is recorded that in 1817 Miss Doughty's residence, The Priory, was surrounded by water for several days. In 1883 the floods reached across the Green and surrounded the churchyard and boats were rowed across the Green to take supplies to marooned householders. The worst flood was probably that of 1928 when the whole village was inundated.

**60.** Here we have a view of Waterloo Place, looking towards the Pond.

**61.** In this view, furniture is being recovered from a flooded house in Defoe Avenue.

**62. LEYBORNE LODGE.** One of the oldest houses in Kew is Leyborne Lodge, which was probably a farm building attached to Brick Farm, part of the Leyborne–Popham estate. It has been in the ownership of the Atwood family since 1820, when Richard Atwood came to Kew to cultivate market gardens between Kew and Richmond. One of his sons was surveyor to the estate and was concerned with the development plans for the area. Atwood Avenue was named after him.

**63. LEYBORNE PARK.** This remarkable scene was painted in about 1830, probably by one of Richard Atwood's daughters. From a position just outside Leyborne Lodge it shows the end of what is now Leyborne Park, looking north across Mortlake Road and along Forest Road—still with its well known sharp bend. The tree at the right hand side still exists in the garden of the Lodge.

**64.   THE HORSE TRAMS.**   From 1883 to 1912 horse trams ran between Kew and Richmond,
from the foot of Kew Bridge to the junction of Church Road and Kew Road, by the Orange Tree.
Two trams are here seen at the Kew terminus in 1899 with the blacksmith's shop in the background.

**65.   THE LAST HORSE TRAM AT RICHMOND IN 1912.**

**66.   THE SINKING OF THE QUEEN ELIZABETH.**   On 5th September 1904, the pleasure steamer *Queen Elizabeth*, the largest and most modern of the river fleet, was making its evening trip from Hampton Court to London Bridge. The tide being low the captain steered through the centre arch of Kew Bridge instead of taking his usual course through the Surrey arch. The vessel struck a submerged pile, left from the bridge works of the previous year, the top of which was only 8″ below the water level. With great skill the captain managed to manoeuvre his badly holed craft alongside Kew Pier and the 200 passengers were able to escape unharmed before the vessel settled on the river bed. The *Queen Elizabeth* had been built in 1895 and was designed to draw only 17″ and it was an amazing chance that she should have met with such a mishap.

**67. QUEEN'S SCHOOL.** The first school in Kew was held in the south aisle of St. Anne's Church when it was extended in 1770. The first separate school building was erected by public subscription on a site adjoining Kew Green and opened in 1826. By command of King George IV it was known as the King's Free School. When Queen Victoria came to the throne the name was changed by her permission to the Queen's School and since then its title has depended on the sex of the reigning monarch. The building shown here, which stood to the north of the Pond, was erected in 1887 and demolished in 1970 after the school had been transferred to the building in Cumberland Road.